MUSE
A Visual Biography

MUSE
A Visual Biography

Narrative by Laura Shenton

WYMER
PUBLISHING
Bedford, England

First published in Great Britain in 2020
by Wymer Publishing
www.wymerpublishing.co.uk
Tel: 01234 326691
Wymer Publishing is a trading name of Wymer (UK) Ltd

Copyright © 2020 Wymer Publishing.

ISBN: 978-1-912782-35-2

The Author hereby asserts his rights to be identified
as the author of this work in accordance with sections
77 to 78 of the Copyright, Designs & Patents Act 1988.

All rights reserved. No part of this publication may be
reproduced or transmitted in any form or by any means,
electronic or mechanical, including photocopying, or any
information storage and retrieval system, without written
permission from the publisher.

This publication is sold subject to the condition that it shall not,
by way of trade or otherwise, be lent, re-sold, hired out or
otherwise circulated without the publishers prior consent in any
form of binding or cover other than that in which it is published
and without a similar condition including this condition
being imposed on the subsequent purchaser.

Every effort has been made to trace the copyright holders of the
photographs in this book but some were unreachable. We would
be grateful if the photographers concerned would contact us.

Design by 1016 Sarpsborg
Printed and bound by Harrier LLC, Newton Abbot, Devon.

A catalogue record for this book is available from the British Library.

ROLL OF HONOUR

Wymer Publishing duly acknowledges the following people who all put their faith in this publication by pre-ordering it:

Robert Abramowicz
Sabino Acito
Jeremy Allen
Gaetano Amato
Max Anacker
Giuseppe Anobile
Leona and Anthony Ashby
Harri Aspfors
Fraser Bathgate
Lydia Beeton
Domenico Bellini
Deborah Bennett
Charles Beterams
Beert Bierma
Gabriele Bigatti
Andy Bingham
Paolo Bonasoni
Alice Bonfà
Marco Bonfanti
Denis Bordin
Gary Bruce
Alan Burton
Yann Cadiou
Suzanne Muse Caley
Pierluigi Capra
Gillian Carson
Luciano Cassulo
Alexis Castaneda
Dave Chalk
Andreas Claus
Nicola Contin
Gavin Costar
Kevin Crisp
Roi Croasdale
Mischa Cronin
Robert Culbert
Annunziata D'Addio
Giancarlo D'andrea
Mark Daniel
Paul Davisson
Simon Denton
Darren DeVivo
Joshua Dieckmann
Andrew Dixon
Serafina Dotto
Donald Dougherty
Trond Dybfest
Jiri Englis

Marzio Fasoli
Paolo Favarato
Massimo Felici
Fabio Figini
Paolo Fiorito
Alex Fishlock
Fabio Flecchia
David Fresno
Michel Gagnon
David Gaylor
Walter Gelormino
Theo Geybels
John Gibbin
Aldo Grassi
Charles Gray
Joe Hall
Thomas Hallstein
William Hayter
Dan Helmbrecht
Sabine Henrich
Mike Hogan
Danny Hogg
Robert Holden
Raffaella Improta
Caroline John
Mark Johnson
Tony Jones
Stephen Lane
Ekaterina Lapina
Jørn-Terje Larsen
James Laughton
Christopher Leith
Stephen Lenhardt
Michael Lewis
Don Lisenby
Paulo Lopes
Lea Maliekhadien
Fabiola Mangano
Aurora Mangolini
Ben Marlowe
Luigi Martinuz
Veronese Maurizio
Diana McCourt
Roberto Minissale
Laura Minò
Sharon Mitchell
Pietrangelo Monte
Benito Muraro

James Murphy
Kees Nijpels
Michael Nix
Dave Osborne
Ian Oxley
Jocelyn Paquette
Massimiliano Patroncini
Manuel Peinado
Fabio Peppoloni
Serafin Perez
Bede Perham
Francesco Piacentino
Sergio Pignata
Ian Potter
Leif Randen
Massimo Reggiani
Libreria Rinascita
David Roberts
Alistair Robertson
Rich Robinson
Sybil Rose
Bernard Rose
Alessandro Roselli
Luciano Rossi
Matteo Russo
Francesco Schembari
Richard Schofield
Partha Sengupta
Matthew Setchfield
Ron Smetek
Mark Solomons
Andrew Songhurst
Gianluigi Sordi
William Spouge
Hannah Spruell
Jerry Stevens
John Stewart
Giuseppe Stipo
Rick Strang
Boris Tessier
Alayna Thompson
Deke Thursby
Bruce Tippen
Marcello Trizzino
Francesco Trotta
Gabriele Vicentini
Fred Vintner
Sami Virtanen

Photo credits: Front cover; P8: ZUMA Press, Inc.; P10: Edd Westmacott; P12 & 13: Fabio Diena; P14 & 15: Edd Westmacott; P34: Jason Moore/ZUMA Press, Inc.; P36 & 37: Jared Milgrim/The Photo Access; P48, 50-53: ZUMA Press, Inc.; P54: Jason Moore/ZUMA Press, Inc.; P56: (top) dpa picture alliance archive; (bottom) Kevin Sullivan/ZUMA Press, Inc.; P64: WENN Rights Ltd; P66 & 67: Rodolfo Sassano; P76 & 77, 78 & 79: Daniel DeSlover/ZUMA Wire/Alamy Live News/ZUMA Press, Inc.; P84 & 85, 86 & 87: Rodolfo Sassano; P88 & 89: Igor Vidyashev/ZUMA Wire/Alamy Live News/ZUMA Press, Inc.; P90, 92 & 93: Roger Garfield/Alamy Live News; P94 & 95: Daniel Karmann/dpa picture alliance archive; P96 & 97, 98 & 99, 100: Axel Heimken/dpa picture alliance archive/Alamy Live News; P102 & 103: KC Alfred/ZUMA Wire/Alamy Live News/ZUMA Press, Inc.; P104, 106-109: SOPA Images Limited/Alamy Live News. (All licensed from Alamy Stock Photo). Back cover and all other images: © Alan Perry Concert Photography.

Formed in 1994 from the gloomy post-Britpop lull, emerged the intergalactic rock band, Muse, all the way from…
Teignmouth in Devon.

Matt Bellamy
(lead vocals, guitar, keyboards)
Chris Wolstenholme
(bass guitar, backing vocals)
and
Dominic Howard (drums).

Matt said, "Something happened when Nirvana died. The whole grunge thing died and England reinvented itself with the Britpop scene… but it became too quirky and English. It became too Union Jack, too insular. It became quirky jokey London Cockney, you know what I mean? It just became a joke. It didn't become about making music. It became about fashion."

When Muse played their first London show in 1995, the Britpop explosion was yet to happen; that was the territory of the Blur versus Oasis competition in the August of that year. It was yet to be that Noel Gallagher would pay a visit to Downing Street in a bid to boost Tony Blair's Cool Britannia PR. Away from all of that; away from what was going on in the mainstream, there was a thriving scene of indie bands playing the small venues in North London. Muse were working away in the background. Small town musicians, Muse had yet to know of the enormous success that they would go on to achieve. That's where their story begins…

Matt said, "Being from a small town makes you look around and immediately see there's no opportunities. If you grow up in a place like that (the city), you've got all these possibilities – you can become a rock star, you can become a journalist. In Teignmouth, you can become a sweet shop owner at best. You learn that from an early age. That gives you this attitude – I've got to do something, I've got to make something out of this place. We were out of touch and uncool compared to what was going on in places like London or Manchester, and that helped us develop something unique."

Matt, Chris and Dominic connected over their shared love of nineties alternative music. Dominic said it was based on, "a lot of Seattle stuff and Rage Against The Machine, Soundgarden even. A lot of that heavy American rock music of the early nineties had a big impact. And then, I think we started rediscovering a lot of earlier influences as kids and I think that's when the film music starts coming back in." Such is evident in the evolution of Muse's sound, Dominic continued, "We started off quite simple and quite raw. And then after the first few albums, we started reconnecting with film music and I think the sound of the band became more and more experimental and more epic the more influences we incorporated into it."

Lyrically, lot of Muse's earlier songs dealt with introspective themes such as relationships, social alienation, and difficulties they had encountered whilst trying to establish themselves in their hometown. However, as the band progressed, the themes featured in their songs have become more diverse to commentate on issues such as the fear of the evolution of technology in their 2001 album, *Origin Of Symmetry*. The 2003 album, *Absolution*, explores ideas about the apocalypse whilst their 2006 album, *Black Holes And Revelations*, has a strong war theme. In 2009, *The Resistance* album focused on themes of government oppression, uprising and love. The album itself was mainly inspired by George Orwell's book, *Nineteen Eighty Four*. In 2012, Muse's sixth studio album, *The 2nd Law*, relates to economics, thermodynamics and apocalyptic themes. The 2015 album, *Drones*, is a concept album that refers to autonomous killing drones as a metaphor for brainwashing and loss of empathy.

As well as George Orwell's *Nineteen Eighty Four*, other books that have influenced Muse's lyrical themes include *Confessions Of An Economic Hitman* by John Perkins, *Hyperspace* by Michio Kaku, *The 12th Planet* by Zecharia Sitchin, *Rule By Secrecy* by Jim Marrs and *Trance Formation Of America* by Cathy O'Brien.

Matt said of his lyric writing process, "You know what? I don't really know what my influences are in terms of lyrics and stuff. I'm more of a sort of music person; when I grew up I'd loved the music so much and I'd listen to the melody and things like that. What was being said in songs was something that never really sort of, I don't want to say they didn't matter too much, but it was never something that really drew me in until I probably came across someone like maybe Tom Waits and Rage Against The Machine as well. They're the

Matt Bellamy, at TJ's in Newport, Wales, 4th September 1999

two sort of lyric writers that made me go, "You know what, actually what they're singing about really makes a huge difference to the feeling of the song, what they're actually saying", that was probably my mid to late teenage years, when I discovered Tom Waits and Rage Against The Machine. It's hard for me to say, my lyrics are nothing like either of those. Whereas what I write myself, usually for me the music comes first. I just try and create a sort of a flow of words that somehow fits with the best melody for the tune or the best expressive feel for the vocal, plus I'm trying to link it to what the music itself is making me feel. So sometimes if I'm writing a tune like 'Take A Bow' on the *Black Holes* album, that's like a pretty weird sort of elaborate sort of sequence of kind of arpeggios and it's very dramatic and classical sounding and very dark as well. That made me lean towards singing about like, you know, what it is to mistrust a political establishment and want to assassinate a president or something weird like that."

Matt continued, "Sometimes the music itself will lead me in and draw out a kind of weird emotion from me that certainly doesn't come out in your every day life. Some of it does end up being autobiographical and I say the stuff ends up being more autobiographical is where the music itself isn't really that kind of dark or weird-sounding on songs like maybe 'Starlight' or 'Madness'. On this album (*Simulation Theory*), like the song 'Something Human', songs where the melodic structure and the chords are relatively simple, it's in those situations where I tend to actually go a bit more autobiographical with the lyrics, like singing about things like love or relationships and things like that. But I'd say Muse, we tend to do songs which have a much more darker musical tone and a much more unusual chordal structure and melody to most traditional pop music and I think for that reason it drawls out of me a lyrical content, which is a bit different to what most people sing about. I tend to go down the route of paranoid anxiety or the impending doom of technology and anxiety about the future of the world and so on. I think some of that stuff actually comes from the fact that that's what the music itself makes me feel when I'm listening to it."

Many of Muse's songs are characterised by vocalist Matt Bellamy's use of vibrato, falsetto, and melismatic phrasing, influenced by Jeff Buckley. As a pianist, Bellamy often uses arpeggios. His compositions often hint at or indeed quote late classical and romantic era composers such as Sergei Rachmaninov (in 'Space Dementia' and 'Butterflies And Hurricanes'), Camille Saint-Saëns (in 'I Belong To You (Mon Coeur S'ouvre À Ta Voix)') and Frédéric Chopin (in 'United States Of Eurasia). As a guitarist, Bellamy often uses arpeggiator and pitch-shift effects to create a more space age type sound. Bellamy has cited Jimi Hendrix and Tom Morello as influences for this. His guitar playing is also influenced by Latin and Spanish guitar music; Bellamy said of the style; "I just think that music is really passionate...It has so much feel and flair to it. I've spent important times of my life in Spain and Greece, and various deep things happened there – falling in love, stuff like that. So maybe that rubbed off somewhere."

Wolstenholme's basslines are a often a central motif in many Muse songs. The band combines bass guitar with effects and synthesisers to create overdriven fuzz bass tones. Both Bellamy and Wolstenholme use touch-screen controllers, often built into their instruments, to control synthesisers and effects. Just some of the equipment used to achieve such effects in their music includes a Korg Kaoss pad and a Digitech Whammy pedal.

15-16th June 2002, Heineken Jammin Festival, Autodromo di Imola, Italy.

Glastonbury 27th June 2004

Glastonbury 27th June 2004

So far Muse have headlined Glastonbury three times, and in 2016 they became the first act to headline each day of the festival (Friday, Saturday and Sunday).

Leeds Festival,
27th August, 2006

With 2006 coming to a close, it was announced Muse would play the newly re-built Wembley Stadium in April 2007. It was sold out within 45 minutes of the tickets going on sale.

Leeds Festival,
27th August, 2006

© Alan Perry

The variety and interest in Muse's music is such that it often gets categorised in many different ways. Described as alternative rock, space rock and progressive rock, Muse mixes sounds from genres such as electronic music, progressive metal and art rock. Within this, forms such as classical music and rock opera are liberally referred to in their work. In 2002, Bellamy described Muse as a "trashy three-piece". In 2005, *Pitchfork* described Muse's music as "firmly ol' skool at heart: proggy hard rock that forgoes any pretensions to restraint... their songs use full-stacked guitars and thunderous drums to evoke God's footsteps." On the band's association with progressive rock, Howard said; "I associate it (progressive rock) with ten minute guitar solos, but I guess we kind of come into the category. A lot of bands are quite ambitious with their music, mixing lots of different styles – and when I see that I think it's great. I've noticed that kind of thing becoming a bit more mainstream."

Throughout their tenure, many of Muse's albums have drawn inspiration from a range of diverse sources. Whilst their debut album, *Showbiz*, brought Muse to prominence, for their second album, *Origin Of Symmetry*, the band wanted to craft a more aggressive sound. In 2000, Wolstenholme said, "Looking back, there isn't much difference sonically between the mellow stuff and the heavier tracks (on *Showbiz*). The heavy stuff really could have been a lot heavier and that's what we want to do with *Origin Of Symmetry*". Their third album, *Absolution*, features prominent string arrangements as well as drawing influence from artists such as Queen. Their fourth album, *Black Holes And Revelations* was influenced by artists including Depeche Mode and Lightning Bolt, as well as a range of Asian and European influences. The band listened to radio stations from the Middle East during the album's recording sessions. Queen guitarist, Brian May, has praised Muse's work, calling the band "extraordinary musicians", who "let their madness show through, always a good thing in an artist."

Muse's sixth album, *The 2nd Law* has a broader range of influences, ranging from funk and film scores to electronica and dubstep. *The 2nd Law* is influenced by rock acts such as Queen and Led Zeppelin (on 'Supremacy') as well as dubstep producer Skrillex and Nero (on 'The 2nd Law: Unsustainable' and 'Follow Me', with the latter being co-produced by Nero). Michael Jackson and Stevie Wonder influences are present on 'Panic Station'; musicians who performed on Stevie Wonder's 'Superstition' make a guest appearance on the song. *The 2nd Law* includes two songs ('Save Me' and 'Liquid State') with lyrics written and sung by bassist, Wolstenholme, who wrote about his battle with alcoholism. It features extensive electronic instrumentation, including modular synthesisers and the French Connection, a synthesiser controller similar to the Ondes Martenot.

Each member of Muse played in separate school bands during their time at Teignmouth Community College in the early nineties. Matt Bellamy successfully auditioned for Dominic Howard's band, Carnage Mayhem, becoming their singer and songwriter. They renamed the band Gothic Plague. They asked Chris Wolstenholme (who at the time was drummer for Fixed Penalty) to join as bassist; he agreed and took up bass lessons. The band was renamed Rocket Baby Dolls and adopted an image that sat somewhere comfortably between goth and glam. Around this time the band received a £150 grant from The Prince's Trust for equipment. This ultimately led to them supporting the Trust through a gig at the Albert Hall on 3rd December 2018.

In 1994, Rocket Baby Dolls won a local battle of the bands contest. Their performance included them smashing their equipment. Bellamy said of the performance; "It was supposed to be a protest, a statement, so when we actually won, it was a real shock,

© Alan Perry

Leeds Festival, 27th August, 2006

Wembley Stadium
17th June, 2007
© Alan Perry

Wembley Stadium
17th June, 2007

© Alan Perry

a massive shock. After that, we started taking ourselves seriously." It was through this that each member of the band quit their respective jobs and changed their name to Muse. The band considered that their newly chosen name of Muse was a good choice due to it being short and that it looked good on a poster. According to journalist, Mark Beaumont, the band wanted the name to reflect "the sense Matt had that he had somehow "summoned up" this band, the way mediums could summon up inspirational spirits at times of emotional need." A move away from Teignmouth promptly followed.

Not being a fan of their hometown of Teignmouth, Bellamy explained, "The only time the town came to life was during the summer when it turned into a vacation spot for visiting Londoners. When the summer ended they left and took all the life with them. I felt so trapped there. My friends were either getting into drugs or music, but I gravitated towards the latter and eventually learned how to play. That became my escape. If it weren't for the band, I would probably have turned to drugs myself." Just as well perhaps then, that all three members of the band are not originally from Teignmouth.

Matt was born in Cambridge on the 9th of June 1978 to Marilyn James and George Bellamy. George was the rhythm guitarist of the English rock group, The Tornados. They were the first English band to have a number one hit in the US. The family eventually moved to Teignmouth when Matt was ten years old.

The Tornados were no longer going by the time of Matt's childhood but George Bellamy's time with the band meant that he was able to offer Matt advice ("Enjoy it while you're young and get laid"). Matt recalled, "Because he (George) had a number one four months after joining the band, he'd had things a lot easier than I did. It was good to be able to talk to someone in your own family to find out what it was like, and people were even more fanatical back then because rock 'n' roll was first coming out. He mainly suggested that I made sure we don't get fucked over and things like that because, I think he did get seriously fucked over."

When Matt was fourteen, his parents got divorced. Matt said, "It was okay at home, middle class, we had money, well until the age of fourteen. I think I almost got everything I wanted until the age of fourteen, yes. Then, everything changed, parents got divorced, and I went to live with my grandmother, and there wasn't that much money. I have a sister who's older than me, she's actually my stepsister

Wembley Stadium
17th June, 2007

– my dad had her from a previous marriage, and also a younger brother. Until the age of fourteen, music was part of my life since it was part of the family circle, my dad was a musician, he had a band, etc. But it's only when I moved in with my grandparents that I started playing music myself. It was like a need to me."

Matt had played the piano since he was six years old, but in the absence of his parents, he started playing the guitar. Matt had an ongoing curiosity in the paranormal. His interest in the Ouija Board increased at the time of his parents' divorce; "It was exciting to go to school and to tell ten year old kids all about it, as they found it all quite scary and I was quite impressed that I was doing something that was scary to other people but that wasn't to me. I did get quite into that." His beliefs changed after one correspondence predicted the first Gulf War a year before it started. "My beliefs in the whole thing changed. I now believe that you're contacting something in your subconscious, which is quite different. Something that you might not have known was already there. That's probably more realistic than thinking you're contacting somebody who's already dead. And I do practice that."

When Matt was younger, he almost learned how to play the clarinet at the request of his parents. He got as far as grade three before giving it up. He also, very briefly, tried violin and piano lessons but he didn't enjoy them. Essentially, Matt is self taught on piano and guitar but it was whilst taking A Level music that he had the opportunity to take classical guitar lessons.

One of Matt's earliest memories in relation to him getting into music was that in 1981, when he was three, he began playing the piano. He used to work out songs from film and TV, note by note, playing by ear, tunes that his brother would encouragingly ask him to have a go at. It started with the theme tune from *Dallas*. Matt soon moved onto stuff by Ray Charles and then popular bands of the time; The Cure, The Smiths and The Wedding Present. Matt said, "For me, music was always associated with fun and pleasure. My parents originally gave my brother piano lessons but he wasn't very good. And because he hated it so much, they never gave me lessons."

Chris Wolstenholme was born in Rotherham, Yorkshire, on 2nd December 1978. His family moved to Teignmouth when he was eleven. His mother would buy records regularly, which would influence him to learn how to play the guitar. Later on, he would play drums for a post-punk band. He eventually gave up the drums to play bass for Matt and Dom.

Dominic was born on 7th December 1977 in Stockport. His family moved to Teignmouth when he was eight years old. He learned to play drums at around the age of eleven, when he was inspired by a jazz band performing at his school.

Dom played drums for a band called Carnage Mayhem when he met Matt. By that time, Matt didn't have a stable band. Naturally, Matt was recruited by Dom and his band members as their guitarist. It was at this time that Chris would meet both Matt and Dom. At the time though, Chris was playing drums for another band in town. In time, Matt and Dom's band fell apart, leaving them without a bassist. Fortunately, Chris gave up playing the drums to play bass for them.

Chris said, "I met Matt and Dom quite a few years before the band started because we went to school together – they were at school ahead of me, but I knew them from seeing them around town. Then a load of bands popped up out of nowhere where we lived – all

Wembley Stadium
17 June, 2007

of a sudden everyone wanted to play the guitar and be in a rock band. I was in a band, Matt and Dom were in another band, but theirs was on the edge of self-destruction and mine was falling apart too, so we got together from there." Matt convinced Chris to join his band by saying "Do you realise your band's going nowhere? Why don't you come and join us."

From the early days of playing together, Matt was interested on writing songs; He didn't want to play covers and by the time they were sixteen, all three had finally formed what was first incarnation of Muse. Prior to calling their band Muse, they had gone by the name of the Rocket Baby Dolls. In this guise, they entered a battle of the bands competition. Matt said, "We were the only real rock band; all the others were pop or funk-pop, kinda Jamiroquai if you want. We knew we had no chance to win - we were not the best musicians - it was a matter of "fitting". So we did the best we could, we took advantage of our feeling of being "different". We came on stage with makeup all over our face, we were very aggressive, we played very violently and then we broke everything on stage. The attitude meant a lot to us. So we won. And I think that psychologically it changed many things in our heads. Because we came to lose, we expected to lose. And we were angry somehow. And we had just realised at this time that we could replace lots of things. We realised that emotion, the vibrations that you create are as important as your technical skills. We had just discovered something: music is a matter of emotion." It was during this time, that the band would name themselves as Muse. Still though, their image changed physically. Matt said, "The first gig we did, we dressed up a little bit like The Cure actually, we tried to look very Gothic, and we had all black makeup on. The band was called Rocket Baby Dolls, it wasn't called Muse. We did this one-off gig, and I think it's the only time we ever did it. After that we just got bored with back-combing our hair."

Muse's early gigs were difficult at the time, they went from playing cover songs in front of fifty people in sport clubs to writing their own songs and doing gigs.

After a few years of building a fanbase, Muse played their first gigs in London and Manchester. They were the supporting band for Skunk Anansie on tour. They had a significant meeting with Dennis Smith, the owner of Sawmills Studio, situated in a converted water mill in Cornwall. He had seen the three boys grow up as he knew their parents. He had a production company with their future manager, Safta Jaffery, with whom he had recently started the record label, Taste Media. The meeting led to their first serious recording session and the release of the Muse EP on 11th May 1998 on Sawmills' in-house Dangerous label, produced by Paul Reeve. Their second EP, the *Muscle Museum* EP, also produced by Reeve, was released on 11th January 1999. It reached number three in the indie singles chart and attracted the attention of British radio broadcaster Steve Lamacq and the *NME*.

Later in 1999, Muse performed on the Emerging Artist's stage at Woodstock '99 and signed with Smith and Jaffery. Despite the success of their second EP, British record companies were reluctant to sign Muse. After a trip to New York's CMJ Festival, Nanci Walker, who at the time was the senior director of A&R at Columbia Records, flew Muse to the US to showcase for Columbia Records' then senior vice president of A&R, Tim Devine, as well as for American Recording's Rick Rubin. It was during this trip that on 24th December, Muse signed a deal with American record label, Maverick Records. Upon their return from America, Taste Media arranged deals for Muse with various record labels in Europe and Australia, allowing them control over their career in individual countries. John Leckie was brought in alongside Reeve to produce the band's first album, *Showbiz*. The album showcased Muse's aggressive yet melancholic musical style, with lyrics about relationships and their difficulties trying to establish themselves in their hometown.

Wembley Stadium
17 June, 2007

© Alan Perry

Wembley Stadium
17 June, 2007

On the gloomy mood of the album, Matt said, "That's the sort of stuff that used to make me feel good. People like Nick Cave – that ridiculous, over-the-top doom, taking it to extremes. I find it uplifting because it's like someone else is feeling what you're feeling and putting it into their music. Someone expressing extreme joy is just as valuable, it's just the fact that they're expressing their soul through music. But I think the first thing that drives people to express themselves is darkness and depression. Our music can definitely be played in the wrong situations. It's definitely made for people to watch it live, but I'm not sure if it's a party-type thing… I wouldn't say we're suburban punks, we're not a bunch of boys who've got everything, whinging about nothing. There is definitely substance behind it, but I don't want to have to go into too much to prove it." At a later point, Matt said, "If anything went wrong in my life, even getting told off by a teacher, I would come home and play music. It would make me realise I'm okay with myself. There are various things that happen in your life, stuff with your family, when you're growing up, and music's always been my escape from that."

Showbiz was recorded between April 1999 and May 1999. However, the album included some older songs from Muse's repertoire, many of which date as far back as 1996. Most of the songs on *Showbiz* had already been written at least by 1997. The songs featured on the album were among the "fifty or so" that Matt Bellamy had written before entering the studio. The band selected the songs for *Showbiz* based on those which they deemed to be the more conventional and "straight-forward". Whilst the songs on the album feature an eclectic and diverse sound with subtle classical, jazz, blues, Latin, and world music influences, there is a distinct and cohesive alternative rock aesthetic. The more experimental material was left out of the album to be included as B-sides on the single releases.

Before they were famous, Muse was often asked to play covers. They hated it. They were determined to play their own music. It went in their favour though. It was on October 1995, that Dennis Smith, had first heard them, in a Cornwall village of all places. Smith said, "Matthew has an incredible range of ideas. He's got such an imaginative and creative mind, which was obvious in those early days, always challenging and wanting to get into very deep conversations that took twenty years of adult life to come to terms with. An older head on much younger shoulders is how I've always seen him."

Some British record companies were reluctant to back Muse on the opinion that that their music sounded too similar to Radiohead. Ironically perhaps, their producer in what would be the early days of their career, John Leckie, had worked with Radiohead as well as the Stone Roses, Weird Al Yankovich and The Verve. On 4th October 1999, *Showbiz* was released around the world, following the success of 'Uno' and 'Cave', Muse's first two singles from the album.

Showbiz was met with a mixed response from local critics. According to some of them, *Showbiz* sounded similar to Queen, Jeff Buckley and Radiohead. *Rolling Stone* magazine gave *Showbiz* three out of five stars, stating that, "*Showbiz* matches Thom Yorke's penchant for majestic agony — screams and the word self-destruction pepper the title track — but with an edge that's quirkier and decidedly more ragged than their elders." *Pitchfork* said of the album that "Muse expertly boil down Radiohead into punkish radio nuggets" but went on to question that "despite this promise, where can they go from here?", which resulted in a rating of six point seven out of a possible ten. In a less favourable review, *NME* advocated that "*Showbiz* is not as clever as they think it is… 'Unintended' and the title track are overwrought, prone to excruciatingly bad pseudo poetry", which

September 15th 2007,
Austin City Limits Music Festival,
Zilker Park, Austin, USA.

resulted in a score of six out of ten. On the other hand, a more positive review was present in *USA Today*, whereby the album was given three out of four stars. It was written that *Showbiz* "offers smart, seductive rock that's sophisticated but not stuffy, fun but not frilly" and that the songs "get a boost from the handsome voice of Matthew Bellamy, who builds tension by vocally snowballing from a hushed intensity to full-throttle wails."

The mixed reviews were certainly not prohibitive to Muse's international success though. 'Muscle Museum' and 'Sunburn' were released as successful singles with 'Unintended' being their first single to hit the top twenty. *Showbiz* showcased Muse's aggressive music style, as well as their emotional style. Some of their songs, such as 'Sunburn', referenced the difficulties they had while trying to establish themselves, as well as lyrical references to love and money. Matt said of 'Muscle Museum', "It's about how different elements of our being – the soul, the body, whatever – won't let another element do what it wants to do, it's about the conflict of not quite knowing what it is you want. Not just relationship-wise, it could relate to the band as well, about how there are still people who will knock you down even though you are down already."

With the success of *Showbiz*, Muse landed spots at big festivals, including the Glastonbury festival (at which they were awarded a gold disc for the sales of *Showbiz*) and the Reading festival. Along with those festivals, a tour of Europe, Australia, and Japan followed. They capped off a successful year with the release of the *Showbiz* box set in France.. They were nominated for Best New Act at the Brit Awards and won the same accolade at the *NME* Awards.

Due to the success of their debut album, Muse were able to secure a considerable fan base throughout Western Europe and thus, after a year of gigs throughout Europe, Muse went back to the recording studio to record their follow-up album to *Showbiz*. John Leckie was approached again to produce their second album, *Origin Of Symmetry*, along with David Botrill. Their second album was considered a change in direction, as Matt explained, "When we did the first album we'd only done a few gigs in London, no major tours. We've learned so much about how we want to be from touring with other bands because of the way they are on stage. If we recorded them in the way other bands do I'd be worried that it would sound the same as them. We've used wind chimes to set up entire backdrops... bits of bones, llama claws and bubble wrap. It sounds much more atmospheric."

Muse developed *Origin Of Symmetry* during their tour for the *Showbiz* album. 'Feeling Good', a cover, was originally written for Broadway by Anthony Newley and Leslie Bricusse in 1964. The song was first recorded by Nina Simone for her 1965 album, *I Put a Spell On You*.

The title of *Origin Of Symmetry* comes from the 1994 book, *Hyperspace* by theoretical physicist, Michio Kaku. It suggests the title of *The Origin Of Symmetry* for a future book about the discovery of super symmetry, a reference to *On The Origin Of Species*. Bellamy philosophised, "Everyone's been writing about the origin of life so now they'll start looking at the origin of symmetry – there's a certain amount of stability in the universe and to find out where it originates from would be to find out if God exists."

9th December 2007
KROQ Almost Acoustic Christmas Gibson Ampitheatre
Universal City.

Origin Of Symmetry was recorded at Ridge Farm Studios in Surrey and Real World Studio in Wiltshire. Additional recordings were made at David Gilmour's Astoria houseboat studio, Richmond Studios, Abbey Road Studios in London and Sawmills Studio in Fowey, Cornwall. The album was mixed at Sawmills and mastered at Sony Music Studios in London.

Musically, *Origin Of Symmetry* has been described as alternative rock, progressive rock, hard rock, and space rock. The album saw the band experimenting with new instruments and dynamics. Dominic Howard expanded the standard rock drum kit with various other items of his own, including a balaphone. The use of animal bones features on the track, 'Screenager'. Matt Bellamy also used an organ at St Mary the Virgin's Church, Bathwick to record 'Megalomania'. Due to the physical requirements of the pipe organ, it is very rare that Muse perform the song live. One of the most notable exceptions perhaps, was at Muse's charity gig at the Royal Albert Hall.

Origin Of Symmetry was released on 18th June 2001 and was met with critical acclaim. The song, 'Plug In Baby' was released as the lead single of the album and reached the number eleven spot in the charts, the highest spot for any Muse single at that time. Their second single, 'New Born', also got into the top twenty. This contributed to the album's respectable chart position at number three. It is plausible that *Origin Of Symmetry* could have been more successful in America but Maverick had reservations about the album's falsetto vocals, which they considered weren't radio-friendly. When Maverick asked Muse to change some of their songs prior to the American release of the album, feeling insulted, Muse departed from Maverick. This move prevented a release of the album in the US at the time.

Origin Of Symmetry was met with generally positive reviews from critics. Q praised it as an "astonishing record... where extra-terrestrial fascinations meet the classical world's more unhinged impulses", adding that "comparisons with Radiohead that dogged Muse's early career now seem all but obsolete." *The Guardian* however, panned the album, complaining that is was "unbelievably overblown, self-important and horrible" in a one-star review. *Stylus Magazine* conceded that Muse "are very good at their craft", but that "the constant overplaying of everything waters it all down immensely." Q later listed *Origin Of Symmetry* as one of the best fifty albums of 2001, whilst *Kerrang!* listed it as the ninth best album of the year.

NME enthused that the album was "amazing for such a young band to load up with a heritage that includes the darker visions of Cobain and Kafka, Mahler and The Tiger Lillies, Cronenberg and Schoenberg, and make a sexy, populist album. But Muse have carried it off." *NME* advocated that, "The inner sleeve of Muse's second album contains an illustration by Darrell Gibbs depicting humans marching into a giant white cube. In tiny lettering above the door, a sign reads "CHAOS". Welcome indeed to the beautiful nightmare world of the most distorting, cartoon intense, baroque 'n' roll band that Britain has ever produced. Here comes their razorblade stuffed-toy singer Matt Bellamy, hanging from the chandelier of his overblown musical ability, electrodes screwed into his brain, singing like a harpy on fire, playing the funeral mass organ with his toes. Here's bassist Chris Wolstenholme and drummer Dominic Howard sounding like Edvard Munch's backing band. And here unfolds the profane, expressionist, hyper-thrilling vista feared by all those hoping the band were just Radiohead with a Freddie Mercury complex. In two years of public life, Muse have accumulated a high-pressured mythology. Half a million copies of their debut *Showbiz* and one iMac advert down the line, they've strewn a totemic trail of destroyed equipment, confessed to a taste for mushrooms, séances and

NIA Birmingham
10th November 2009
The Resistance Tour

© Alan Perry

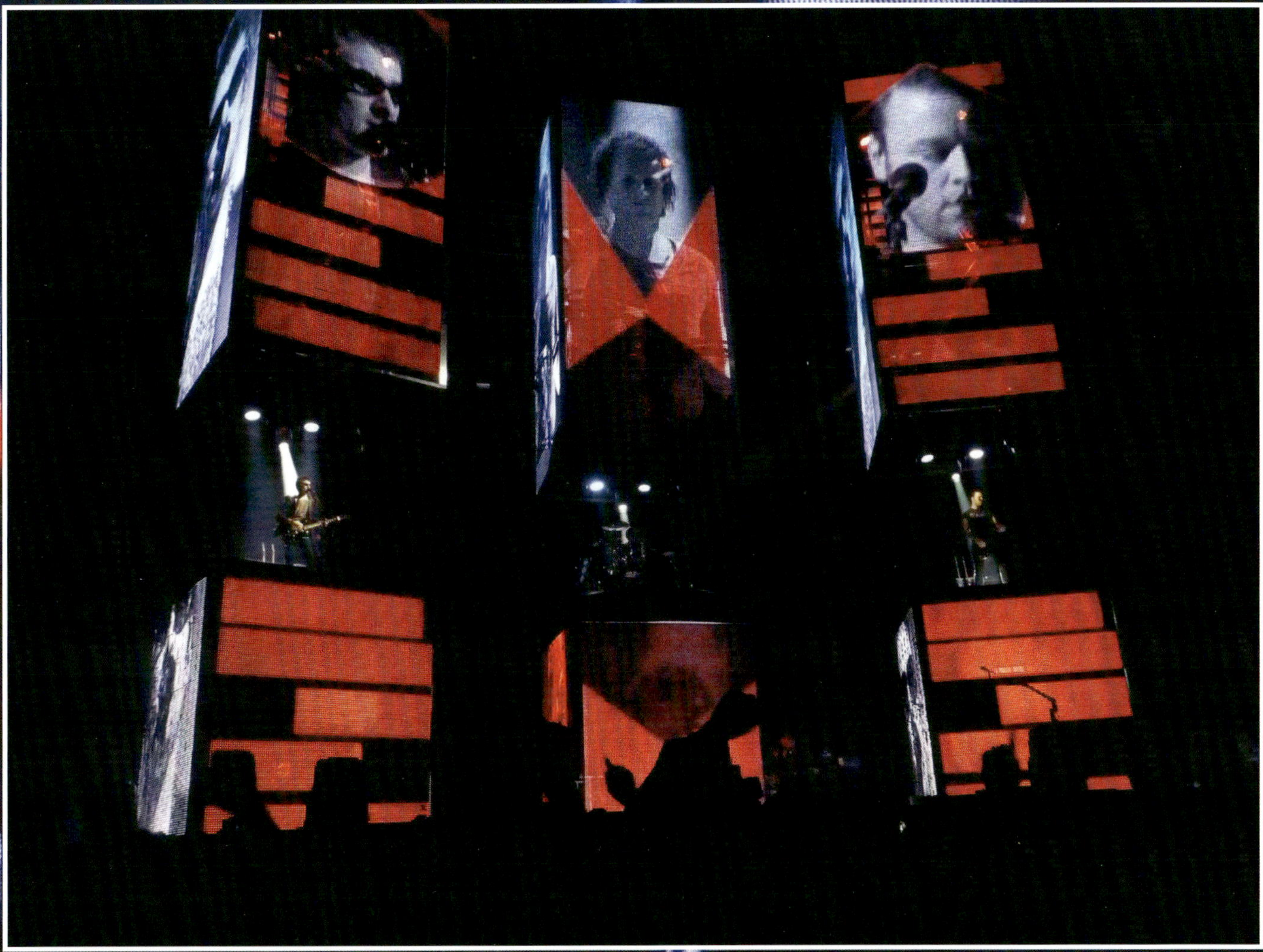

41

NIA Birmingham,
10th November, 2009
The Resistance Tour

© Alan Perry

NIA Birmingham,
10th November, 2009
The Resistance Tour

© Alan Perry

NIA Birmingham,
10 November, 2009
The Resistance Tour

© Alan Perry

April 17, 2010, Coachella Valley Music and Arts Festival. Indio, California; USA.

Hector Berlioz's 'Grande Messe Des Morts' and announced, "If I couldn't do this I would not want to live." The stakes were high. Their reinvention of grunge as a neo-classical, high gothic, future rock, full of flambéd pianolas and white-knuckle electric camp, is a precarious venture. Yet as the bloody abattoir riff kicks in on 'New Born', colliding with Bellamy's fairy dreamtime piano, it's apparent that Muse can handle their brutal arias."

Origin Of Symmetry proved to be heavier and darker than *Showbiz*, and showcased Matt's falsetto vocal technique. It also strongly featured his distinctive piano playing, as was inspired by the works of Rachmaninov and Chopin, Matt's favourite composers. As well as his heavy guitar riffs being present on the album, it also featured Muse's willingness to experiment with more unorthodox instruments; a church organ, Mellotron and animal bones. Their second album resulted in Muse winning multiple awards, such as Best British Act at the *Kerrang!* Awards, as well as nominations for three Q Awards, which were Best Album, Best Live Act, and Best Producer. The release of the album was also followed by a world tour, which included visits to Australia, Japan, Germany, Austria and France. Muse released two more singles before releasing another album, which were 'Bliss' and a double A-side, 'Hyper Music'/'Feeling Good'.

On 1st July 2002, Muse released a two-disc album containing multiple B-sides and live versions of some of their songs. This was accompanied with a release of a DVD containing a documentary and a live performance in Paris, which they considered to be their best gig to date at the time. As Matt advocated, "Towards the end of touring *Origin Of Symmetry*, we played our biggest gig at the time in Paris. We felt that we were playing our best gigs then, and agreed that we should capture it. The first album was a bit of a grind, a lot of doubt, but we'd approached the second album with a positive carelessness both in terms of the album and the touring. We felt that we had to remember that. We brought along one of our mates who'd lost his job, so he became the party organiser and documented a lot of it on video camera. At the time I felt all that wasn't going happen again, coming out of yourself and reaching that moment of freedom that you really want. I think a lot of people get in bands without wanting to be famous or successful – a lot of it is about wanting to be free of the constraints of society. That was what I experienced at the time." Both entitled *Hullabaloo Soundtrack*, this proved to be a moderate success. Along with this release was the release of an EP in France and Japan, entitled *Dead Star* EP, which featured the double A-side from *Hullabaloo Soundtrack*, 'Dead Star'/'In Your World' as well as a cover of Franki Valli's 'Can't Take My Eyes Off You'. Muse topped off a high flying year by winning Best Live Act at the *Kerrang!* Awards, as well as selling 1.3 million copies of *Origin Of Symmetry* globally.

Muse took a break from touring to record their third album. They dropped John Leckie as their producer and worked with Paul Reeve, John Cornfield, and Rich Costey. Matt said of Costey, "He was the man we originally thought of working with for the rock tracks. He'd previously mixed some great rock records - Audioslave, Rage Against The Machine's *Renegades*, The Mars Volta - but in the meantime he'd been sending us discs of other people he'd worked with like Philip Glass and Fiona Apple and was trying to convince us that he should do the whole album. We reworked 'Apocalypse Please' with a more aggressive sound, without too much over-production, and it sounded better. In the end he did do pretty much all the album, and mixed it as well. He understood what we were trying to achieve. The main thing with Rich was that his mixing technique was pretty precise. Every cab would have about ten microphones on it and they would all be placed with mathematical precision. I remember spending a whole day playing the guitar and seeing Rich outside with a measuring tape and a spirit level! He was making the slightest adjustments, millimetres at a time to get it so there was perfect phase."

April 17, 2010, Coachella Valley Music and Arts Festival. Indio, California; USA.

Muse began *The Resistance tour* in Teignmouth in September 2009. The tour included headlining Coachella festival in April 2010.

April 17, 2010, Coachella Valley Music and Arts Festival. Indio, California; USA.

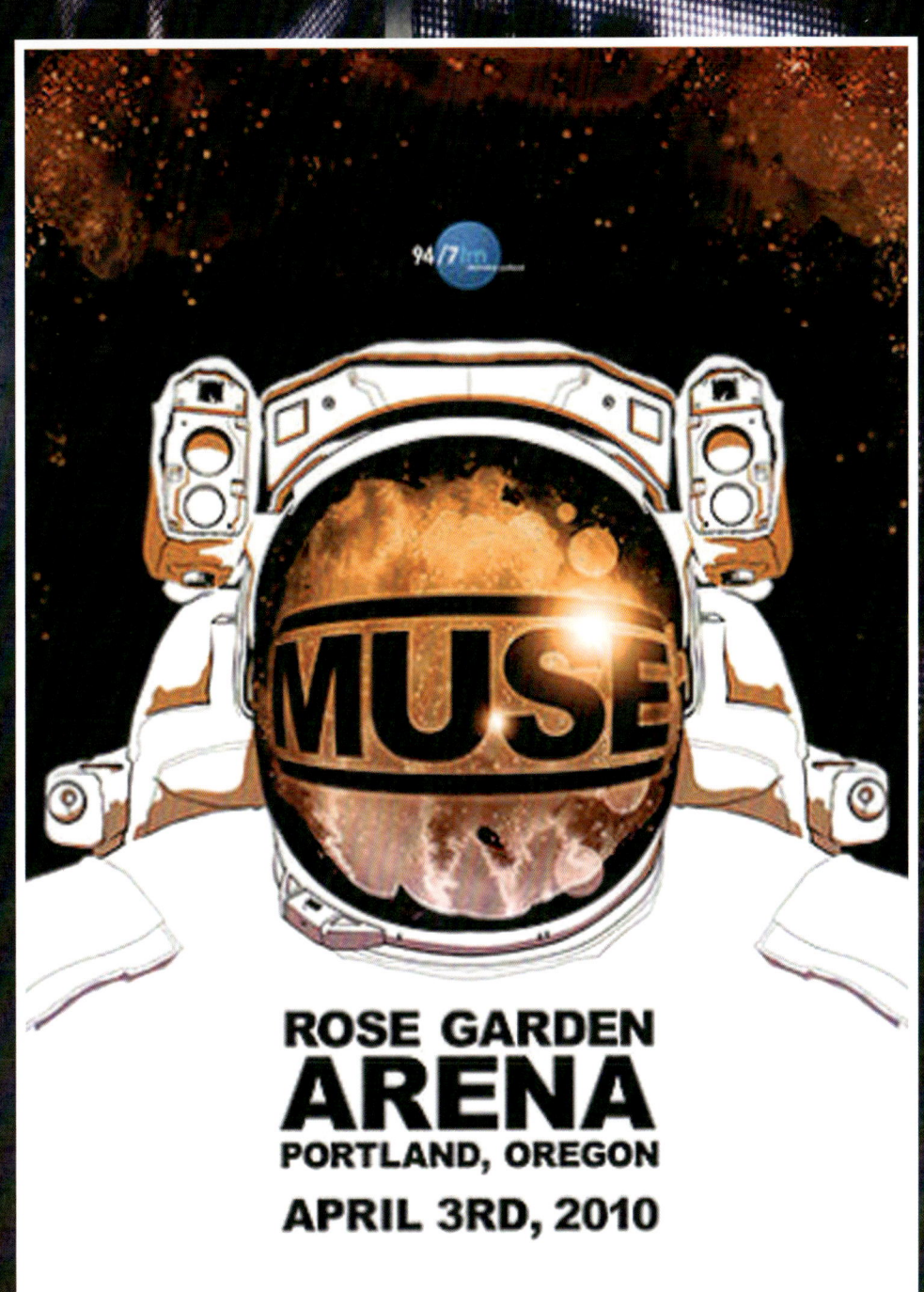

21 November 2010. Muse receive an award for Favorite Alternative Rock Music Artist at the 38th Annual American Music Awards in Los Angeles, California, USA.

On the left, Tom Kirk steps in for the absent Chris. Tom is the band's media manager. He arranged and edited footage for their video releases Hullaballoo and the Absolution Tour and he also runs the official website.

Grammy Awards
February 13, 2011

Muse's initial remit for their third album was that they wanted it to feel emotionally uplifting. However, the political events regarding the US and UK going to war at the Gulf and Iraq changed all of that. Matt said, "We started off with a full orchestra, experimenting, pushing it right over the Queen mark – ninety eight backing vocals, thirty two piece orchestra and all sorts! We did two songs like that and kinda lost our minds. We ended up deciding to get back to basics. We re-recorded some of the stuff with the orchestra, toned it down a little bit. It sounds a lot harder now than I expected. In terms of general context, the world's changed in the last year, the world events of the last year and a half. It's not that we're a political band but I think it's impossible to avoid those things. I think there's a lot of apocalyptic stuff going on in a lot of the songs. While we were recording all the war (with Iraq) was coming out and we were in the process of recording while watching that. The direction definitely took a pretty harsh change in the middle of it all. In relation to the album, it's come across more as a general fear and mistrust of the people in power. It's about moments of extreme fear, and a fair bit of end of the world talk."

Matt explained how different he intended the third album to be compared to *Showbiz* and *Origin Of Symmetry*; "In the past I was layering guitars quite a lot but this time I wanted to get just one guitar part to stand out and be just perfect. On the last album for example, on songs like 'Citizen Erased' or 'Micro Cuts', I did a lot of multiple guitar parts. But when I went to do it live, I actually found myself simplifying the guitar parts and found that the simple parts were much more effective and much more powerful sounding. So in making this album, instead of recording the songs in layers, I was actually working on the parts a lot more before I recorded them."

After months of experimentation, recording, and mixing, *Absolution*, Muse's third studio album, was released on 29th September 2003. It was met with critical acclaim. *Absolution* featured Muse's continuation of blending classical influences into their hard rock style of music, with songs such as 'Butterflies And Hurricanes' and 'Ruled By Secrecy'. Unlike their previous albums, *Absolution* featured a very dark theme – the end of the world. This theme was often portrayed on the album through the lens of Matt's ongoing interest in conspiracy theories, theology, science, futurism, computing and the supernatural.

NME advocated of *Absolution*; "In our green, moneyed corner of Planet Earth, possibility is being pissed up the wall. For the vast majority of human beings, at the age of about twenty one, the sparkle in the eyes deadens just a little, reason overtakes wonder, and they become a citizen rather than a soul. As the prophet Ally Sheedy foretold in the third greatest film ever made, *The Breakfast Club*, "When you get old, your heart dies." Yet for a few sacred people, that disengagement from the simple and the obvious is never quite total. Their eyes will always be that little bit wider than everybody else, and these are the people with the equipment that might lead them one day to genius. For Muse lynchpin Matt Bellamy, those years banging his head against a brick wall are over. He's broken through, found a better place on the other side, and he wants us all to come with him. Just minutes into *Absolution* he sets down his ultimate commandment to this lazy world, on thunderous opener 'Apocalypse Please'. "It's time," he says, "we saw a miracle." Muse's third album is packed full of them. The trappings of showbiz, muscle museums and plug-in babies have all been cleared away – swept under the carpet as childish things. Free of fripperies like detail, reference or circumstance, Bellamy has put together a collection of simple, poetic, transparent songs that re-engage with the old words and values; honour, courage and righteousness. It's one long love letter to

The NEC, BIrmingham,
30th October, 2012
The 2nd Law tour

© Alan Perry

The NEC, Birmingham,
30th October, 2012
The 2nd Law tour

The NEC, BIrmingham, 30th October, 2012
The 2nd Law tour

7th December 2012. Matt with his then fiancée Kate Hudson leaving the Groucho Club, London after celebrating Dom's birthday.

the Impossible Dream, and it WILL NOT SURRENDER. There's been no record released yet this century with stakes so high. Musically, it could have been a disaster. But one man's prog is another man's progress, and every guitar here sounds like it's from the future, every flourish and movement scored and orchestrated with the celestial vision. By indulging every pomp rock wet dream he's ever had, Matt's found that there's no such thing as too much distortion, and that, when you care this much, chartbusting tunes really do fall from the sky."

Along with the release of this album, Muse released two singles, 'Stockholm Syndrome', which was a download-only single from their website, and 'Time Is Running Out', which proved to be their breakout hit, reaching the number eight spot in the UK charts.

Their third album signified the point at which Muse reached mainstream critical acclaim in Britain. With a new American record deal, the band started their first international stadium tour. It included gigs at Australia, New Zealand, the US, Canada, France and Iceland.

At the end of a successful 2003, Muse released another single, 'Hysteria', which received critical acclaim due to its pounding bassline. The song has become a staple track for the band and they won the Q Innovation Award as well as Best Album and Best British Band at the *Kerrang!* Awards.

At the beginning of 2004, Muse continued touring the world. Their stops included Australia and Japan. Chris lost his wedding ring in Japan and it was eventually returned to him by a fan. Other tour stops included France and the US. During a small gig in Atlanta, Matt was injured; he was accidentally hit with his guitar when they started to play 'Citizen Erased'. The gig was stopped at once. Matt recalled of the event, "I didn't feel any pain at first. Then I spat out this liquid and there were gushes of red stuff spurting out all over the microphone. I ran backstage and started puking up. At first you could feel the stitches stretching my face as I sang but now the only problem is that they seem to be disappearing into my lip." Dom recalled, "I knew it was bad as soon as he turned around, there was blood dripping everywhere."

Fortunately, Matt recovered in time to continue their North American tour, with a stop at the Coachella Valley Music Festival, as well as stops in Utah, Toronto, and Vancouver. *Absolution* was a certified hit in North America. 'Sing For Absolution' was released as a single at the eve of their huge European festival tour. It was yet another Muse single to reach the top twenty.

Whilst touring, Matt got into playing Poker. He said, "I'm really into the mind games of poker. I'm more ruthless than the other two so I've been taking all their money. It can get boring. In Barcelona I had to go to a casino to play with some pros. I still made around 500 Euros. You know the Channel 4 poker programme, *Late Night Poker?* My ambition is to appear on that. But the stake is £1500 and I'm not quite good enough yet."

Muse began their big festival tour in Europe with a stop at the Pinkpop Festival, as well as the Rock am Ring and the Rock im Park in Germany. On 27th June 2004, Muse headlined the Glastonbury Festival. This performance featured a fantastic set from them. They ended the memorable night with the song, 'Stockholm Syndrome'. Matt described this gig as "the best gig of our lives" during their set. Poingantly, just mere hours after headlining Glastonbury, tragedy struck. Bill Howard, Dom's father, died from a heart

November 16th, 2012
The Unipol Arena, Bologna, Italy
The 2nd Law tour

The Ricoh Stadium, Coventry
22nd May 2013
The 2nd Law tour

attack after attending the festival to see them. "It was the biggest feeling of achievement we've ever had after coming off stage", said Matt, "It was almost surreal that an hour later his dad died. It was almost not believable. We spent about a week sort of just with Dom trying to support him. I think he was happy that at least his dad got to see him at probably what was the finest moment so far of the band's life." With support from his band mates and his family, Dom decided to stay with the band and continue with the tour. Their next single, 'Butterflies And Hurricanes' was dedicated to his father.

As the tour carried on to the US with the Cure Curiosa tour, Chris injured his wrist in a collision with The Cooper Temple Clause bassist, Didz. It happened while they were playing football. The injury put a number of festival date possibilities in doubt. However, a temporary replacement was found in Morgan Nicholls, bassist for the UK hip-hop act, The Streets. With Chris playing keyboards and providing backing vocals, they managed to continue their tour, with an iconic show at the V Festival in August. The tour continued with a stop at Australia prior to Muse touring the rest of North America. Muse began to play new material during this part of the tour. During this tour, Muse won the Best Live Act at the Q Awards, two MTV Europe Music Awards for Best Alternative Act and Best UK/Ireland Act, and another Best Live Act from the UK Festival Awards. Muse ended their spectacular year with two special Christmas gigs at Earls Court. Both gigs sold out.

At the beginning of 2005, while Matt was on holiday at the Kingdom of Bhutan, Chris and Dom picked up Muse's Brit Award for Best Live Act. They also won an *NME* Award in the same category. Muse's award tally was growing every year at such rate.

Muse continued their tour in April with several gigs in the US for MTV's Campus Invasion tour. During this tour, Muse played four new songs while heavily mixing their setlist. The four new songs were named with anagrams on the setlists as a puzzle for fans to solve. It eventually became two treasure hunts, which led to fans winning bikes signed by Muse. 'Stockholm Syndrome' was also released in America as the third single from *Absolution*, despite it being initially released two years ago as a download-only single.

Muse ended their touring for that year with a performance at the historic Live 8 concert in Paris. They were originally scheduled for only the London leg. Not long after, the *Absolution* box set, containing all of their singles from the album of the same name, was released in France. Around this time, Muse were finally able to release *Origin Of Symmetry* in the US with a new record deal under Warner Music. This became possible after the band had completed their contractual obligations with Taste Media.

Whilst on a long break from touring, Muse used the time to record new material for their fourth album, produced again by Rich Costey. They started recording at the Miraval Studio in France. However, problems with the management, as well as with ghosts and bats (yep!) caused them to move their recording to New York. It was in New York that the majority of content for the album was completed. As with *Absolution*, Muse were able to take their time recording their fourth album. With no pressing deadlines or events in their schedule, the time was theirs to play with in terms of creatively, being able to do something different. According to Chris, they worked on one song at a time, and if they liked it, they kept it. While recording, Muse won another award – the MTV Woodie Award. Muse also released another DVD, the *Absolution Tour* DVD. The DVD features their headlining Glastonbury set, re-edited and mastered. Footage from their Earls Court shows are also present. By this time, *Absolution* had sold one million copies in Europe.

The Ricoh Stadium, Coventry
22nd May 2013
The 2nd Law tour

The Ricoh Stadium, Coventry
22nd May 2013
The 2nd Law tour

The Ricoh Stadium, Coventry
22nd May 2013
The 2nd Law tour

© Alan Perry

17th May, 2015.
The KROQ Weenie Roast Y Fiesta at Irvine Meadows Amphitheatre in Irvine, California.

17th May, 2015.
The KROQ Weenie Roast Y Fiesta at Irvine Meadows Amphitheatre in Irvine, California.

Dublin, 5th April, 2016
The Drones tour

After spending half a year recording and mixing, Muse released their fourth album, *Black Holes And Revelations*, on 3rd July 2006. The album was very well received. Unlike their previous albums, *Black Holes And Revelations* featured a wide range of alternative music themes, from classical to techno. And that's just the tip of the iceberg! On what inspired him during the making of the album, Matt said, "I've been listening to quite a lot of music from the south of Italy I've been living in Italy for a while, and I discovered this music from Naples, which sounds like a mix of music from Africa, Croatia, Turkey and Italy. It kind of gives it a mystical sound, so I think that's one thing that influenced the album. I like being influenced by things that have a mixed style."

Black Holes And Revelations also made reference to more of Matt's interests; conspiracy theories, space, Mars and Cydonia, the *Book Of Revelation* and the Four Horsemen of the Apocalypse. According to Matt, the overriding theme of the album is based on the feelings of tension and fear that hang over the world. He explained, "The fifties was an era of worldwide tension, of nuclear fear and of war. Today, we've come back to this feeling, like at the end of a cycle. There's even been a rise in the interest in space. This theme, the connection between current tensions and those from long ago, can really be heard on the album." Alongside the release of the album was the release of its first single, 'Supermassive Black Hole', which reached number four in the UK.

On the album, producer, Rich Costey, wanted to capture Bellamy's personality as a guitarist. Costey explained, "I wanted to make a record where you could hear his fingers on the strings, and you could hear his pick hitting the strings." Bellamy said it was the first time that Muse made an album without being concerned about how they would play it live; It was also the first time they learned about studio technology, having previously left it to the engineers. The 'Map Of The Problematique' riff was written on a keyboard. At Costey's encouragement, Bellamy recreated it on guitar by splitting the guitar into three signals, which were processed with pitch shifters and synthesisers. 'Soldier's Poem' had originally been written for *Absolution* but it was rewritten for *Black Holes And Revelations*. The new lyrics and new arrangement was inspired by 'Can't Help Falling In Love' by Elvis Presley. Dominic Howard said they were originally going to record 'Soldier's Poem' with a "massive, epic" approach, but then decided to strip it down and record it in a small studio with vintage equipment and a few microphones. Muse were pleased with the result and Howard described it as a "real highlight", enthusing that the song contained "some of the most amazing vocals I've ever heard Matt do".

NME conceded of *Black Holes And Revelations*, "Britain's grandest rockers boldy go where no band has gone before" where it was advocated of the album; "So, just how bombastic, overblown, wilfully obscure, magnificent, portentous, histrionic, eccentric and mental is Muse's new record? Well, there's a moment, as 'Hoodoo' morphs into epic finale 'Knights Of Cydonia', when a piano that sounds like it's heralding the destruction of the universe gives way to the sound of galloping horses. Horses! It's as if the Four Horsemen themselves have come from the underworld by the closing seconds of track ten. Then there's laser guns, explosions and sirens before a choir of deathly damned begin a dreadful, unearthly wail. It's *The Book Of Revelations* gone rock, and it's the most overblown thing in the world. Except it's not this world: Cydonia is the region of Mars where evidence of pyramids and oceans are the best clue to prove there was life there once. Toto, I don't think we're in Albion anymore…

Barking stuff, obviously, but why does music have to be so serious, so authentic? Rock is the only art form where authenticity is held supreme – more important than moving

Dublin, 5th April, 2016
The Drones tour

Dublin, 5th April, 2016
The Drones tour

14th May 2016.
Mediolanum Forum, Assago Milan Italy.

On 15th February 2016, *Drones* won Best Rock Album at the 58th Grammy Awards.

14th May 2016.
Mediolanum Forum, Assago Milan Italy.

18th July, 2017
Toronto, Ontario, Canada

18th July, 2017
Toronto, Ontario, Canada

or provoking you. It's as if the whole rock canon has been assembled by a committee of sociologists rather than hedonists, madmen and geniuses. When did using the imagination become a crime? Muse are classic whipping boys for the Keeping It Real campaigners, having never written songs about bouncers, waiting for taxis or fancying girls on dancefloors. Why bother with, say, the shonky (sic) bits of Sheffield when you've got the entire cosmos to sing about?"

Muse began touring again. They kicked things off with a performance at BBC Radio One's, One Big Weekend, in which they performed a few songs from the new album as well as songs from previous albums. Matt, Chris, and Dom were somewhat nervous about this performance. As Matt explained, "We're a little bit rusty obviously, but we'll give it our best shot. We are looking forward to playing – it's good to do a gig after such a long break. It sort of kicks our arse back into gear and er, yeah, I'm looking forward to it. We'll probably play a few new tracks there, and obviously a couple of old ones as well, and yeah – I'm looking forward to it."

Following this performance and various promotional TV appearances, Muse continued on their tour. It consisted of mainly festival appearances, with a notable headlining slot at the Leeds and Reading festivals, which would be one of the highlights during their tour. Chris said, "The biggest highlight for me was headlining Reading last year. We went there as kids and I think it was ten years to the day that I saw Rage Against The Machine play – and that was one of the best gigs I'd ever seen! Their show has embodied my perception of Reading ever since, so to be on the same stage headlining ten years down the line was a pretty good feeling. Out of all the festivals in Europe, Reading is the best rock crowd you're ever going to get. No matter what time of day you're on, you know the crowd are going to be mental – you don't get that at any other festival." The tour continued with several dates in North America throughout the summer. It was during this leg of the tour that Muse released another single, 'Starlight', which proved to be the band's biggest hit in America. It reached number two on the US modern rock chart. Muse later began a large arena tour of Europe, with three sold out dates at Wembley Arena. During their tour of Europe, they released another single in the UK, 'Knights Of Cydonia', which was described as "six minutes and one second of pure genius." Whilst touring, Muse won more awards at the MTV Europe Music Video Awards; Best Alternative Act and Best Live Act. During the awards, Justin Timberlake commented that Muse was the best band there when he introduced them prior to their performance of 'Starlight'. Also, Brandon Flowers, lead vocalist of The Killers, mentioned Muse while they received the Best Rock Group award. Muse spent the rest of the year touring Europe.

With 2007 approaching, it was announced that Muse would be the first band to play in the newly-rebuilt Wembley Stadium, on 16th June. Following the announcement, the first night was sold out in just forty five minutes. This prompted the organisers to schedule another show for the 17th June.

Muse began 2007 with a tour of South East Asia and Australia, with a headlining slot at the Big Day Out festival. During their tour of South East Asia, Muse won the BRIT Award for Best Live Act. They were also nominated for Best Album and Best British Band, but they lost to the Arctic Monkeys. In March 2007, it was announced that Muse would not be the first act to play at the newly-reconstructed Wembley Stadium. Instead, it would be singer George Michael who would be the first act to play in the 90,000 capacity stadium.

27th August, 2017
Reading Festival, Reading

27th August, 2017
Reading Festival, Reading

3rd June, 2018
Rock im Park open air festival,
Zeppelinfeld, Nuremberg, Germany

21st September, 2018
Reeperbahn Festival, Hamburg, Germany

Muse's eighth studio album Simulation Theory was released on 9th November 2018.
The Simulation Theory World Tour started in February 2019.

21st September, 2018
Reeperbahn Festival, Hamburg, Germany

21st September, 2018
Reeperbahn Festival, Hamburg, Germany

Muse's 2007 world tour continued onto the US, with dates supporting punk band, My Chemical Romance. After a show in Williamsburg, Virginia, members of My Chemical Romance's band and crew, as well as Muse's, suffered from severe food poisoning. It resulted in the cancellation of several shows. This prompted fans of My Chemical Romance and Muse to send death threats to the chef who served the food.

Despite the unfortunate blip, the tour carried on once everyone was feeling better, with headlining spots at the Rock am Ring, Rock im Park, Pinkpop Festival, and the Isle of Wight festival. During such performances, Muse surprised their fans by playing old songs, including 'Micro Cuts', 'Blackout' and 'Unintended', which made its return to the setlist after a six year absence.

For their Wembley gigs, Muse invited several bands to support them. The result was that they turned the whole thing into another summer festival. For the night of the 16th, The Streets, Rodrigo y Gabriela and Dirty Pretty Things were the supporting acts and for the 17th, there was My Chemical Romance, Biffy Clyro, and Shy Child as the support acts. After their Wembley gigs, Muse continued their tour with stops that included Monaco and France. It was announced not long after, that they would also tour America again, with a gig at the world's most famous arena, Madison Square Garden. The Cold War Kids were invited to be the supporting act on this American tour.

Muse's fifth album, *The Resistance*, was released on the 14th September 2009. It was the first Muse album produced by the band themselves. The album was engineered by Adrian Bushby and mixed by Mark Stent. It topped the album charts in nineteen countries and became the band's third number one album in the UK. It also got to number three on the Billboard 200. Critics were mostly positive about *The Resistance*, with much of the praise directed towards its ambition, classical music influences and the thirteen-minute, three-part 'Exogenesis: Symphony'.

The first single, 'Uprising', was released seven days before the album was. It included a remix of the title song by Does It Offend You, Yeah?, as well as 'Who Knows Who', a collaboration with The Streets. However, the first song released from the album wasn't 'Uprising', it was 'United States Of Eurasia', but this was only available as a free download from the official Muse website once a treasure hunt puzzle had been completed. Joe Ellis became the first DJ to air the new song on KXLL during his Sunday show on 19th July 2009. It was following the conclusion of the treasure hunt on 21st July 2009 that the song was made available for download, complete with ending piano sonata 'Collateral Damage', a slightly altered version of Frédéric Chopin's *Nocturne in E-flat Major*, with additional sounds of children at play and a line of jet fighters dropping nuclear bombs at the end of the piece.

NME published a pre-release interview with the band on 7th July, identifying 'United States Of Eurasia' as one of the highlights of the album and describing how it "builds into a climax of multi-tracked Queen-style vocals."

The Resistance was reviewed by the BBC in 2009; "Less earnest and self-regarding than Radiohead and less free trade-hippie than Coldplay, Muse know exactly how guilty a pleasure they can be. Stuffing their albums with sing-along pomp and circumstance, their days as sub-prog pariahs have long since passed. Comparing *The Resistance* with its 2006 predecessor, *Black Holes And Revelations*, is never going to be easy. The latter was an audacious leap into the hallowed area where cosmic meets commercial in a way not seen

5th March, 2019
Pechanga Arena, San Diego, California, USA
The Simulation Theory world tour

28th March, 2019
Scotiabank Arena, Toronto, Canada

since *Dark Side Of The Moon*. There is a distinct development here, but a self-produced heaping on of classical motifs and Queen-style histrionics isn't necessarily the one we were hoping for. It's not that they're taking themselves too seriously, more that you're never sure if the listener is supposed to.... Quoting Chopin or Saint-Saëns verbatim isn't necessarily maturation either, but time and again Muse remind you of how good they are at making your pulse race."

Muse began The Resistance tour in Teignmouth in September 2009. The tour included headlining Coachella festival in April 2010. Other headlining festival slots in 2010 included Glastonbury (due to U2 having to cancel their headline slot following Bono's back injury - U2 guitarist, The Edge joined Muse to play the U2 track, 'Where The Streets Have No Name'), Oxegen, Hovefestivalen, T In The Park, Austin City Limits and the Australian Big Day Out. It also included two gigs at Wembley Stadium in September 2010. Muse also supported U2 for their U2 360° tour. Between September and November, Muse toured North America. Muse provided the lead single for the film, *The Twilight Saga: Eclipse*, 'Neutron Star Collision (Love Is Forever)', released on 17th May 2010.

For their live performances, Muse received the O2 Silver Clef Award in London on 2nd July 2010. It was presented to them by Roger Taylor and Brian May of Queen; Taylor described the trio as "probably the greatest live act in the world today." On 12th September 2010, Muse won an MTV Video Music Award in the category of Best Special Effects for the 'Uprising' video. On 21st November, Muse won an American Music Award for Favourite Artist in the Alternative Rock Music category. On 2nd December, Muse were nominated for three accolades for the 53rd Grammy Awards. The ceremony took place on 13th February 2011, during which Muse won Best Rock Album for *The Resistance*.

Based on having the largest airplay and sales in the US, Muse were named the Billboard Alternative Songs And Rock Songs artist for 2010 with 'Uprising', 'Resistance' and 'Undisclosed Desires' achieving 1st, 6th and 49th respectively on the year end Alternative Song chart. On 30th July 2011, Muse supported Rage Against The Machine at their only 2011 gig at the LA Rising festival. On 13th August, Muse headlined the Outside Lands Music And Arts Festival in San Francisco. They also headlined the Reading and Leeds festivals in August 2011. To celebrate the tenth anniversary of their second studio album, *Origin Of Symmetry*, the band performed all eleven tracks. Muse also headlined Lollapalooza in Chicago's Grant Park in August 2011.

In an April 2012 interview, Matt Bellamy said that Muse's next album would include influences from acts such as French house duo, Justice, and UK electronic rock group, Does It Offend You, Yeah? It was on 6th June that Muse released a trailer for their next album, *The 2nd Law*, with a countdown on the band's website. The trailer, which included dubstep elements, was met with mixed reactions. On 7th June, Muse announced a European Arena tour, the first leg of *The 2nd Law* tour. The leg included dates in France, Spain and the UK. The first single from the album, 'Survival', was the official song of the London 2012 Summer Olympics and Muse performed it at the Olympics closing ceremony.

The second single, 'Madness', was released on 20th August 2012, with a music video put out on 5th September. Muse played at the Roundhouse on 30th September as part of the iTunes Festival. *The 2nd Law* was released worldwide on 1st October, and on 2nd October 2012 in the US; it reached number one in the UK albums chart, and number two on the

28th March, 2019
Scotiabank Arena, Toronto, Canada

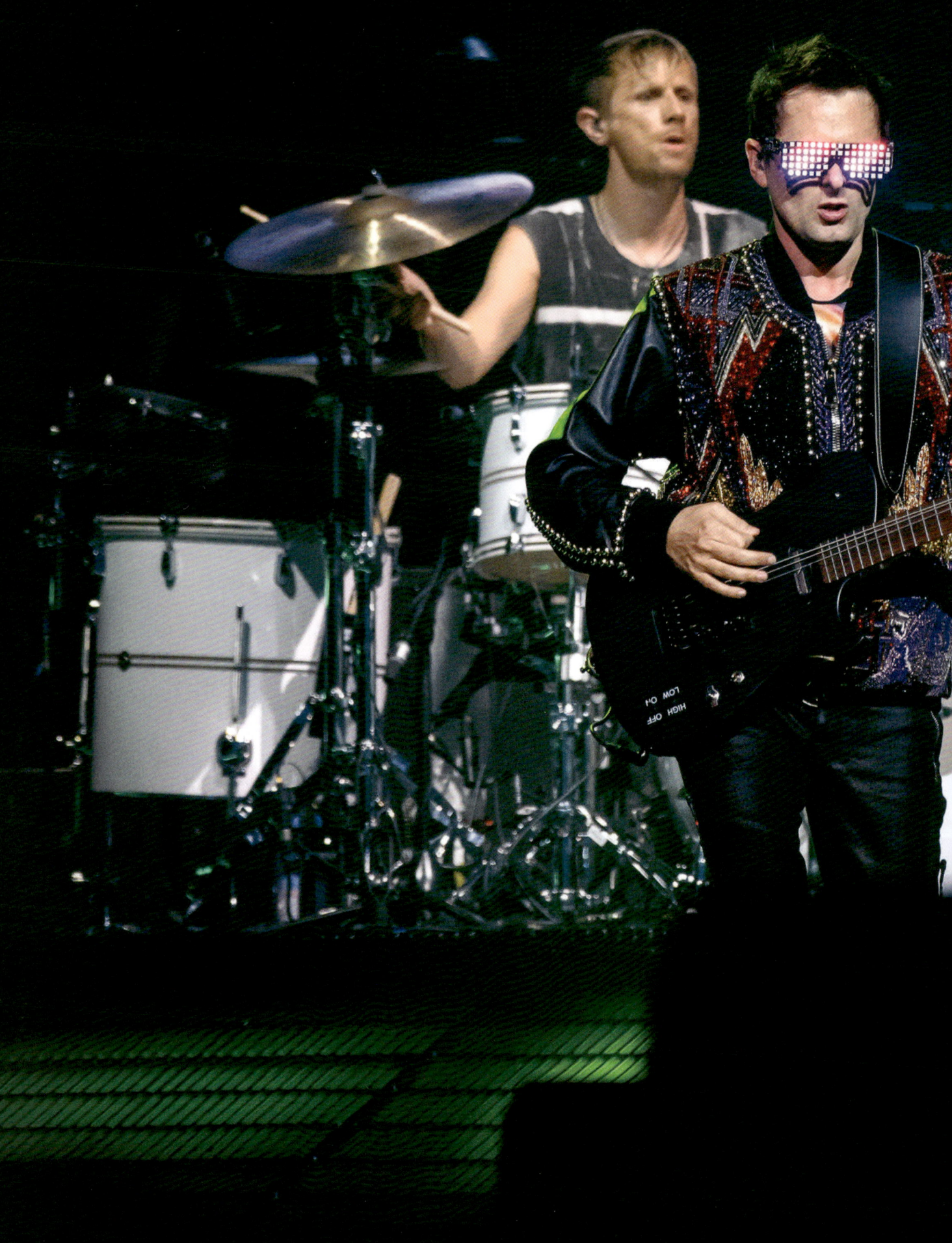

28th March, 2019
Scotiabank Arena, Toronto, Canada

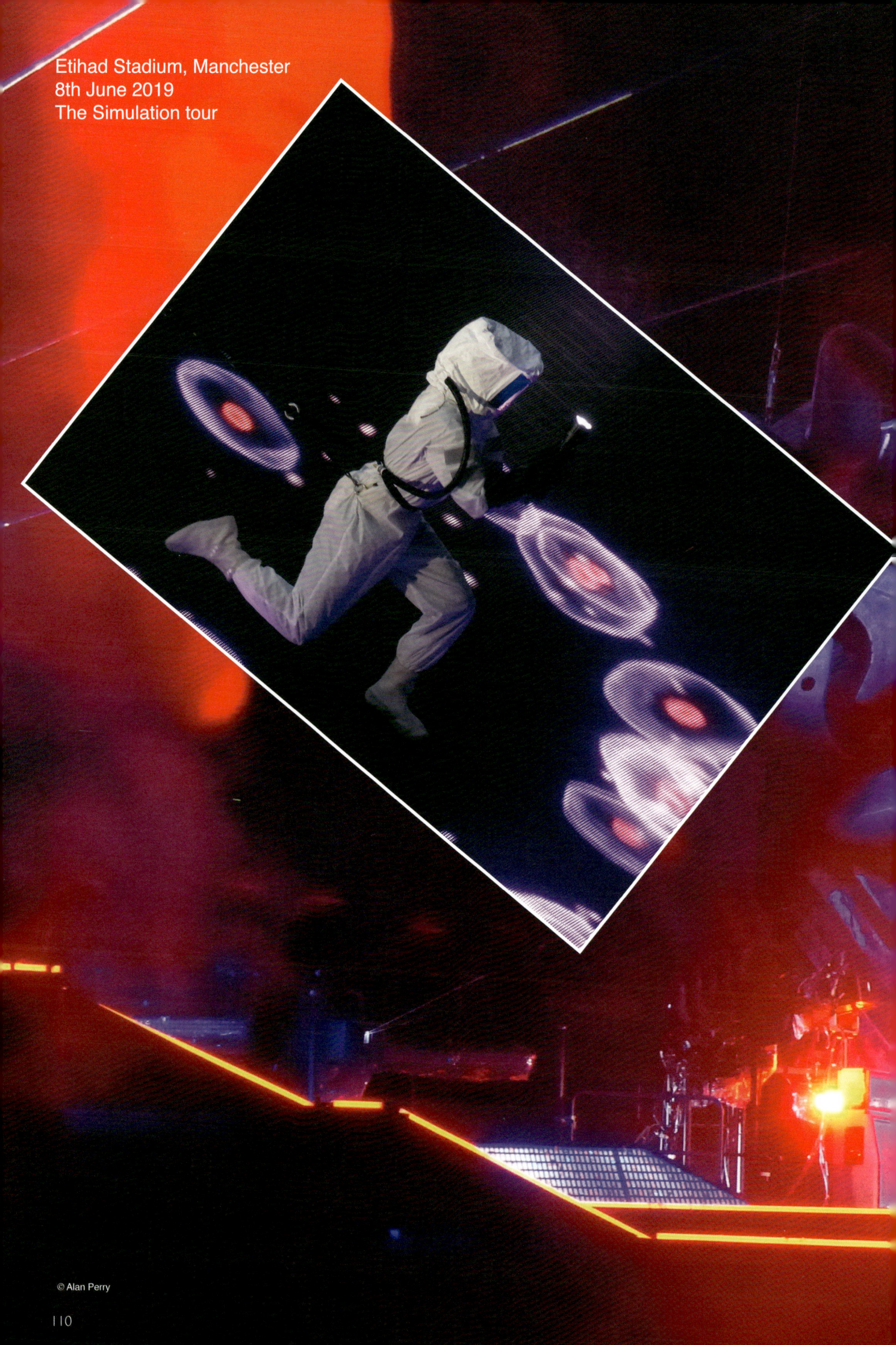

Etihad Stadium, Manchester
8th June 2019
The Simulation tour

© Alan Perry

Etihad Stadium, Manchester
8th June 2019
The Simulation tour

© Alan Perry

Etihad Stadium, Manchester
8th June 2019
The Simulation tour

US Billboard 200. 'Madness' earned a nomination in the Best Rock Song category and the album itself was nominated for the Best Rock Album at the 55th Grammy Awards, 2013. The album was listed at number forty six on *Rolling Stone's* list of the top fifty albums of 2012 whereby it was advocated; "In an era of diminished expectations, Muse make stadium-crushing songs that mix the legacies of Queen, King Crimson, Led Zeppelin and Radiohead while making almost every other current band seem tiny."

Overall, *The 2nd Law* was a top ten-charting album in thirty one countries and a number one album in thirteen countries. The album has been certified platinum by the BPI in the United Kingdom, the FIMI in Italy, the IFPI in Switzerland, and the MC in Canada. It has also been certified triple-platinum by the SNEP in France.

During the recording of *The 2nd Law*, Bellamy jokingly described the album as a "Christian gangsta rap jazz odyssey, with some ambient rebellious dubstep and face-melting metal flamenco cowboy psychedelia" on his Twitter account. In an interview with *Kerrang!* on 14 December 2011, Wolstenholme stated that the album would be "something radically different" from their prior releases. He also said that it felt as if the band were "drawing a line under a certain period" of their career with their sixth album. In another interview, Chris mentioned that the band had been particularly experimental when working on the album.

The album also contains explicit lyrics, making *The 2nd Law* Muse's first album to feature the Parental Advisory label. Bellamy revealed that during the recording of *The 2nd Law* he was reading the Max Brooks novel, *World War Z*, which became a major influence on the album, especially on the tracks 'The 2nd Law: Isolated System' and 'Survival'. 'The 2nd Law: Isolated System' was featured in the film adaptation of the novel.

The 2nd Law was reviewed in *Pitchfork*; "Muse released the trailer for *The 2nd Law*, it was the kind of pre-emptive shock tactic you typically expect from a record that has a lot riding on it. "MUSE GOES DUBSTEP!!!" created a minor firestorm, albeit one that was containable because it was utterly predictable. Of course Muse fans would storm the YouTube comment section with bloodthirsty vengeance. However you think Muse fits into the lineage of Queen or Rush musically, they've benefited greatly from establishing themselves as a last bastion of technically boastful and very popular prog-rock that's always implicitly held unkind attitudes toward synthesiser-based music. On the other hand, of course Muse would eventually glom onto EDM. It's the last frontier for a band that's only now integrating those sandworm basslines but whose music has always provided listeners with equivalents of "the drop" - a glass-shattering falsetto run, Wagnerian crescendos, solos that are gunning for the one tab per month in *Guitar World* that's from the last decade."

Muse released their fourth live album, *Live At Rome Olympic Stadium*, on 29th November 2013 on CD/DVD and CD/Blu-ray formats. In November 2013, the film had theatrical screenings in twenty cities worldwide. The album contains the band's performance at Rome's Stadio Olimpico on 6th July 2013 that took place in front of over 60,000 people. It was the first concert filmed in 4K format. The concert was part of the Unsustainable tour, Muse's mid-2013 tour of Europe.

Muse began writing their seventh album soon after their performance in Rome. The band felt that the electronic side of their music was becoming too dominant; they wanted to return to a more simple rock sound. After self-producing their previous two albums, the

Etihad Stadium, Manchester
8th June 2019
The Simulation tour

© Alan Perry

Etihad Stadium, Manchester
8th June 2019
The Simulation tour

© Alan Perry

band hired producer Robert John "Mutt" Lange. This was done in order that they could focus on performance and spend less time mixing and reviewing takes. Recording took place in the Vancouver Warehouse Studio from October 2014 to April 2015.

Muse announced their seventh album, *Drones*, on 11th March 2015. The following day, they released a lyric video for 'Psycho' on their YouTube channel. They made the song available for instant download with the album pre-order. Another single, 'Dead Inside', was released on 23rd March.

From 15th March to 16th May, Muse embarked on a short tour of numerous small venues throughout the UK and the US as part of their Psycho tour. Live performances of new songs from such concerts are included on the DVD accompanying the album, along with bonus studio footage. On 18th May 2015, Muse released a lyric video for 'Mercy' on their YouTube channel, and made the song available for instant download with the album pre-order.

Drones was released on 8th June 2015. It is a concept album about the dehumanisation of modern warfare. It returned to a simpler rock sound with less elaborate production and genre experimentation. It topped the album charts in the UK, the US, Australia and most major markets. Matt Bellamy said of *Drones*, "To be honest, *Drones* was probably the first album that we'd done that we thought "this is easy", that was a real step backwards in a way - and I don't mean that in a bad way - but it was the most retrospective album we've done. We really made a conscious effort to eliminate all the external influences outside of rock, and really strip it back to the basics. That was a really easy album for us to play live - I remember going into rehearsals for that album and we played it as we did in the studio, and that was it."

Drones was reviewed in *Pitchfork*; "Like their prog-pop predecessors Rush, Queensrÿche, and Pink Floyd, Muse will never be cool, but their subject matter will always be relevant - they only deal in current events that speak to timeless pathologies of the human condition. *The Resistance* raged against any and all machines while the environmentally conscious *The 2nd Law* made global warming appear to be yet another shadow government conspiracy rather than scientific fact. Likewise, *Drones* is not a critique of American military strategy, but rather, "the journey of a human, from their abandonment and loss of hope, to their indoctrination by the system to be a human drone, to their eventual defection from their oppressors." Really, what are Muse records but blockbuster action flicks centred around a cryptocratic nightmare that can be explained on a billboard?"

The Guardian referred to *Drones* as an "Owellian breakup album"; "Since Black Sabbath's 'War Pigs' and 'Iron Man', hard rock has enjoyed warily eyeing the interface between robotics and warfare, themes generally untouched by the more house-trained species of pop music. For their seventh album, Teignmouth trio Muse have grasped this paranoid sub-genre with both hands, riffing on a tendency already glimpsed on albums such as 2009's *The Resistance* and 2003's *Absolution*. Never a band to shy away from a prog-rock statement, Muse's *Drones* is a concept album about remote killing machines, dehumanised drones in thrall to authority – psychotic soldiers, and the rest of us – and the possibility of sedition through love. It's heavy on Orwellian vibes, the grand gestures of Queen, and the fancy fretwork of singing guitarist Matt Bellamy, whose neuroses about control (or, really, his lack of it) have sold a tidy 17m albums to date, making Muse one of the biggest rock bands in the world, one who finally found themselves on the cusp of cracking the US with their last album, 2012's *The 2nd Law*. The whole album is meant to be a back-to-

Etihad Stadium, Manchester
8th June, 2019
The Simulation tour

© Alan Perry

basics exercise, stepping away from extraneous string sections and EDM, one that none the less finds room for a closing chorale (the title track), a speech by John F Kennedy decrying the sneaky methods of communists, and a ten minute, several-part denouement called 'The Globalist', in which our hero seems to go nuclear."

Muse headlined Lollapalooza Berlin on 13th September 2015. On 15th February 2016, *Drones* won Best Rock Album at the 58th Grammy Awards. On 24th June, Muse headlined the Glastonbury festival for a third time, becoming the first act to have headlined each day of the festival (Friday, Saturday and Sunday). On 30th November 2016, it was announced that Muse were to headline Reading and Leeds 2017.

Muse's live show at London's O2 Arena was reviewed in *The Guardian* in 2016; "At the start, the security staff appear like menacing cyborgs, fanning out in the photographers' pit. At the end, after 'Knights of Cydonia' – Muse's portentous, gleeful set closer – singer Matt Bellamy's grand piano is swallowed up by the ground, along with him. This is Muse, winners of umpteen best live band awards, in their natural habitat – a wide bowl, for the third of their five London dates. All told, their *Drones* world tour gives impeccable arena. A long, horizontal stage sets Muse up in the round, circumnavigating drummer Dominic Howard (and touring member Morgan Nicholls on keyboards). Bellamy and bassist Chris Wolstenholme prowl hither and yon on the two runways as lights strafe them. During 'The Handler', a malevolent puppet-mistress projection controls them with strings. The songs are meaty, precise and loud, recalling Queen to U2 to Marilyn Manson (the glam stompers, chiefly). The riffs from Led Zeppelin's 'Heartbreaker' and AC/DC's 'Back In Black' are quoted. Wolstenhome bats a giant confetti-filled balloon away with his bass."

In 2017, Muse toured North America. They were supported by Thirty Seconds To Mars and PVRIS. Howard confirmed in the February that the band were also working in the studio again. On 18th May, Muse released 'Dig Down', the first single from their eighth album. In November, they performed at the BlizzCon festival.

'Thought Contagion', the second single, was released on 15th February 2018, accompanied by an 1980s-styled music video. In June, Muse opened the Rock in Rio festival. On 24th February, they played a one-off show at La Cigale in France with a setlist that had been voted for by fans online. Matt said at the time, "Only people who are going to the show can vote. Unless we've been hacked, and now I can see the songs that have been picked, I wonder if we have been hacked by some crazy fan somewhere." Muse's manager, Peter Mensch, was certain that fans would pick the obvious choices. But that wasn't to be. As Matt said, "He (Mensch) told us, "Don't worry, all they're gonna do is pick well known songs", I said to him, "You don't know our fans!" - turns out they've picked way more obscure songs than even I imagined. Most of them are B-sides and at least two of them are songs we've never even performed live before." A concert video, *Muse: Drones World Tour*, was released in cinemas worldwide on 12th July 2018.

On 19th July 2018, Muse released 'Something Human', the third single from their upcoming album at the time. Matt said of the song, "Life on the road can bring out your inner beast, this song and video is about taming that beast, desiring a return to something human." On 30th August 2018, they announced their eighth studio album, *Simulation Theory*. It was to be released on 9th November. The announcement was accompanied by another single and video, 'The Dark Side'. The fifth single, 'Pressure', was released on 27th September. The Simulation Theory world tour began in Houston on 3rd February 2019 and concluded on 15th October in Lima.

Etihad Stadium, Manchester
8th June 2019
The Simulation tour

Matt said of *Simulation Theory*, "This is probably a 50/50 blend of electronic programming and organic instruments, and even that, by modern standards, is pretty retro. The vast majority of top forty music is just laptops and a vocalist, and even the vocalist is largely processed. We're still flying the flag as best we can for humans making music rather than programmers. We live in the age of the programmer… the individual auteur, often not social, outgoing people, these are the people very much dominating the scene. We're trying to create this symbiosis between the absolute cutting edge of programming and technology, but still trying to find a place for humans. That's the entire journey of Muse."

'Dig Down' was one of the first songs written for *Simulation Theory*. It is a reaction to the social and political climate following the Brexit referendum and the 2016 US presidential election. 'Thought Contagion' was written in late 2017 following Muse's move to LA. The verses stem from Bellamy's anxieties surrounding his observations of the American news at the time. The chorus alludes to Bellamy's concerns about the power that misinformed or ideological people have over their audiences. The title of the song was inspired by scientist, Richard Dawkins, who compared the spread of thoughts "regardless of their accuracy and truth", to a viral disease.

NME advocated of *Simulation Theory*; "With the artwork of *Simulation Theory* designed by *Stranger Things* artist, Kyle Lambert, and each of the videos so far showing them entering virtual reality recreations of different times and realms, Muse are very much decamping to the imaginations of their childhood bedrooms. Following the blacker-than-black war-mongering dystopia of 2015's *Drones*, they have found an escape from the mire of the here and now."

As a live act, Muse are still very much at the top of their game. Their performance at the Royal Albert Hall was reviewed in December 2018 by *NME*; "Last night saw Muse play a special charity show at London's Royal Albert Hall, performing songs from new album *Simulation Theory* live for the first time as well as a medley consisting of '15 minutes of metal'. The show was in aid of the Prince's Trust, with frontman Matt Bellamy informing the crowd that the gig had raised over half a million pounds. Streamed via the band's Instagram, the show saw the audience invited to sing Happy Birthday to bassist Chris Wolstenholme, who was also married at the weekend. Opening with the live debut of 'Algorithm', Muse also aired the titular 'Showbiz' from their debut album, as well as playing the-funk metal new song 'Break It To Me' live for the first time, along with a medley of '15 minutes of metal' consisting of sections from some of their heavier material, with 'Stockholm Syndrome', 'Assassin', 'Reapers', 'The Handler', 'Dead Star', 'Micro Cuts', 'New Born' and 'Ashamed'."

On 7th September 2019, exactly twenty years after the release of their *Showbiz* album, Muse announced the *Origin Of Muse* box set, to be released on 6th December 2019. At the time of writing, it is known that it will include remastered versions of *Showbiz* and *Origin Of Symmetry* on CD and vinyl, along with CDs of demos, B-sides, and live performances, including forty previously unreleased tracks. The box set is also said to come with a book of setlists, posters, photos, original artwork and an interview.

Since Muse signed to Maverick Records and released their debut album, *Showbiz*, in 1999, showcasing Bellamy's falsetto and a melancholic alternative rock style, they have had success after success; both in terms of the albums and singles they have released, the tours they have done and the many plethora of awards that they have won.

Etihad Stadium, Manchester
8th June 2019
The Simulation tour

To date, Muse has moved with the times in their music. Matt Bellamy said, "I don't think we're set on anything. The music industry has changed, and people have changed with it. In a way, I think that's why the last fifteen years has been such a weird time of uncertainty for a lot of people, because there's been a way of doing things for such a long time - in terms of people working in album cycles - and I guess the way that the industry works now, and the way that people listen to music now, means that the idea of cycles isn't as relevant as it used to be. You're not really promoting an album anymore, because people don't buy albums anymore - you're effectively using your album as a means to promote the band in general."

Muse have always embraced technology, both in their music and their live stage shows. Matt Bellamy said, "We've been very lucky in that the band has coincided with this era of technology development, in terms of both music and visual. I think back to the first album, when we had no production - we were just a band on stage with a few lights. Around the *Origin Of Symmetry* time, it was the first time we had a screen, but it was a proper old-school projector, effectively a piece of plastic rolled down at the back of the stage. We've grown through this time now… HD was a big thing. All of a sudden, being able to have these big screens. And then 4K! It's almost like every time we've gone on tour that there's been this whole new bunch of technology available to use that even three or four years previous to that would've seemed unthinkable. That's something we've always tried to do, and not even just with the basics of HD or 4K. For instance with *Drones*, the actual drones themselves, that flew around the arena - that was something that had never been done in a live show, and was brand new technology that had just become available and that we really wanted to push. I'm sure now when we start exploring what's available, there will be a whole bunch of new stuff. As long as you're aware of what's available and what's happening, closely watching everything as it's in development, there's always lots of new things that you can do. I think for us, we were thinking that maybe we can step away from that a little bit and try and enhance the performance side of the show. That's something we've never really done. In 2013, when we did the stadium shows, we started to bring in a couple of performance elements, but it was quite basic. We had a couple of actors that came on for a couple of songs. We quite liked that, but it wasn't enough of a thing. We've been talking about really trying to explore that avenue now."

On the subject of staying current, Matt Bellamy said in 2018, "The challenges are largely the same. It seems like every two or three years the world is a different place so we've always attempted to make rock still have a meaning or a purpose or a sense of being. We are trying to bring technology and the instruments that we play together to create a symbiosis rather than opposing forces. And because the technology is always changing and the political landscape is always changing, the language we have to work with is changing all the time, as well. It is definitely more lonely than it used to be. I feel like in the 2000's there were so many contemporaries that we had an affinity with, or a friendly competitive spirit with, and that's missing now. But also it gives us the feeling that we are doing something relevant - because we are a dying breed, you know?"

Much of the musical excitement of Muse is in their willingness to embrace a range of styles and genres. They are experimental. Their second album, *Origin Of Symmetry*, incorporated wider instrumentation and romantic classical influences, and earned them a reputation for energetic live performances. *Absolution* continued to embrace classical influences via the use of an orchestra on tracks such as 'Butterflies And Hurricanes'. *Black Holes And Revelations* incorporated electronic and pop elements, displayed in singles such as 'Supermassive Black Hole' The album brought Muse wider international success. *The*

Etihad Stadium, Manchester
8th June 2019
The Simulation tour

© Alan Perry

Resistance and *The 2nd Law* explored themes of government oppression and civil uprising and cemented Muse as one of the world's major stadium acts. Their seventh album, *Drones*, was a concept album about drone warfare and returned to a harder rock sound. Their eighth album, *Simulation Theory*, prominently featured synthesisers and was influenced by science fiction and the simulation hypothesis. Throughout their entire discography, Muse have been prolific in offering many points and avenues of musical interest.

© Alan Perry